I0461945

Business Dissertation:

By improving the work-life balance for employees, are organizations able to increase staff retention?

By Jabeir Ahmed

Contents Page:

Abstract

The topic work-life balance explores different types of methods of flexible working and schemes that are family friendly which will give employers wider choice type of work. This would allow those that do not want to work full time, permanent employment and would like to have the opportunity to have both work and their many aspects of their lives combined together according to Beardwell et al (2001, pg105).

The main Objectives for this were to research into many different published

materials on the work life balance topic. Therefore materials such as journals,

articles, books and websites to garner a firm understanding about it. The

literature review and its findings from it created a hypothesis which can be

tested upon many methods of primary research to gain conclusions about the

effects of work life balance ideologies and policies have on staff retention. Also

recommendations will be looked at which will identify options and improvements

that organisations can make to increase staff retention and improve work life

balance.

Also there were many methods of primary research used and these are focus

groups which were done using people of 2 differing age groups. This helped to

support other methods of research by garnering questions which can be used to

create questionnaires. These questionnaires were given to 2 companies such as

TK Maxx in Balham and also to a local pharmacy in Tooting. Both management

and employees were involved in taking part of the questionnaire which

developed quantative data that was then used as key analysis. Another key

source of research was a structured interview with questions asked about work

life balance policies at TK Maxx and also views and opinions of the interviewees

about the policies of work life balance in the work place.

The conclusion is that work life balance does affect staff retention and was

looked at the moist effective policies through both primary and secondary data.

Also structures of an organisation of work life balance policies which improved

the relationships with their employees were given using the most effective strategy to do this successfully. Therefore the organisation and employee bond

will be the strongest and most effective incentive if employees are to remain in

the organisation.

Introduction

The main purpose of this project is to see if improving work life balance of employees are organisations able to increase staff retention. Work life balance is described by Clutter buck (2003) as having the awareness of the demands of time and energy, having the ability to make choices of allocation of both time and energy, recognising the values that apply to those choices made and also making choices.

Schemes of work life balance look to have a positive impact of employees which will allow staff to have control in the way they work along with the things they do outside of it. Chartered institute of personnel and development have surveys which shows that 3 out of 4 people say it would be hard to work any harder than they do, as well as 1 in 5 people say that they take work to their homes daily. Looking at this published material by CIPD and their results from the survey gives a clear understanding of the increase in interest in the problems that work life balance has. Also people have issues with having their commitments outside of work being in the way because of the demands of work.

Furthermore an important aspect of the purpose of the research is the relationship between work life balance and staff retention, in which Manfred Kets De Vries states that "high performers are like frogs in a wheelbarrow, as they can jump out of it anytime", (Williams, pg.28). In order to increase staff retention, methods of doing so are very important because it can help reduce costs of having to recruit and train staff and instead keep the hard working key staff within the organisation.

It is a great deal to outline the importance of this topic because organisations see work life balance as a key component now of the importance of having to provide employees with work life balance in order to encourage upon job satisfaction, therefore it is again important to outline the relationship between work life balance policies and staff retention.

Also Organisations need to identify importance of job satisfaction and work life balance so that it is viable to create the policies that will help staff retention within the organisation by keeping the employees. By looking at published material for motivation, it can give indications why people do what they do. For many decades there have been many studies on motivation and the ideas of it in which both work life balance and flexibility at work have been developed. Herzberg is a great example who refers to motivation and satisfaction as "we can expand by stating that the job satisfiers deal with factors involved in doing the job, whereas he job dissatisfiers deal with factors which define the job context", (Herzberg, 1959). Which simply put was that satisfiers were the motivators and the dissatisfiers were the hygiene factors. A few decades ago there were theories developed based on flexibility and work life balance. The UK based on flexibility and work life balance has centred on the flexible firm model which was initially developed by Atkinson in 1982. (British Journal of industrial Relations, By Arne L. Kalleberg (2001). This model was created to be used as a solution for problems in a work place environment.

Literature review

The primary objective of this review is to research different materials and publications of work-life balance to create an understanding on whether or not organizations will be able to increase staff retention as well as improving the work-life balance of the employees. It will also help to understand how they are applied into organizations. Also by critically assessing theories and contributions of work life balance, findings were discovered which are very significant as to whether improving work-life balance increase staff retention.

The topic work-life balance explores different types of methods of flexible working and schemes that are family friendly which will give employers wider choice type of work. This would allow those that do not want to work full time, permanent employment and would like to have the opportunity to have both work and their many aspects of their lives combined together according to Beardwell et al (2001, pg105).

In an article by NHS, the Shetland NHS has a work life balance program for their employees. This has been done as they understand and recognize that there can be an impact on employee's social lives because of their working lives. Therefore the Shetland NHS board has introduced a program that will help balance both work and life.

The program consists of emergency family leave. This is granted on the basis of an employee's dependant is ill, injured, assaulted or giving birth, or a breakdown and also death which could be either to attend or arrange a funeral. Secondly Special leave is granted in terms of a short term leave i.e. an unforeseen emergency that needs attending urgently. Parental leave is given to a person who is responsible for a child. The Shetland NHS allows 13 weeks of unpaid leave if a child is under age of 5. If a child is older such as 14 then leave is allowed up to 18 weeks unpaid depending if the child is receiving disability allowance. Thirdly Maternity leave and paternity are both given as all companies and organizations do. This is granted to someone who is pregnant and takes time off to be ready for the birth of their child and paternity leave is the partner of a pregnant woman in which case they are given leave to be with their partner.

Other pregnancy related leaves include unpaid contractual leave, sickness leave due to illness because of child birth, miscarriages, pre term birth.

A lot of organizations have indeed generated money into effort and time into initiatives and many policies to improve work life balance. Also the Shetland NHS gives examples which show great work life balance policies. This shows that putting in the time and effort along with investing money in trying to achieve good work life balance for employees can work. This would also mean organizations therefore can keep their best employees and also recruit the best meaning an increase in staff retention.

Furthermore it is necessary and important to analyze secondary data critically in a detailed and justified manner because it will enable to have indications of the qualities and faults of the literature. The best way to critically review analysis effectively is by set judgment criteria according to Dees (2000).

The set judgment criteria are as follows according to Dees (2000) for literature analysis:

The author an expert who is recognized in motivation and work-life balance?

Are the findings supported and what elements oppose the ideas?

Is the research laid out in a logical manner and also is there valid enough evidence?

The chosen hypothesis should he judged.

Is the author making a point of fact or an opinion?

Using these techniques along with flexible working practices and motivational

employee frameworks which underline this topic of work-life balance can then be

analyzed in order to find the key components and arguments for this research.

A theory which underlines the basic needs of people is Maslow's hierarchy of

needs. The theory is based on meeting people's core needs such as the balance between work and life along with it providing a classification of human needs

and category relationship.

Below is the model – **Maslow's hierarchy of needs (1954)**

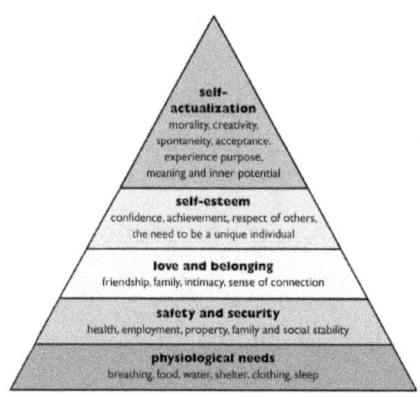

Physiological: Person would start at the bottom of this pyramid and want to satisfy their basic needs. When these needs have been satisfied and fulfilled they would not be a motivational factor and would pursue the next level.

Safety and Security: This is based on physical safety and protection of employment to keep their job.

Social needs/love and belonging: This is where individuals want to be part of a type of group for e.g.

this is based on love, belonging and wanted and friendship.

Self Esteem: Self esteem needs are referred to as being given recognition for their work. This could be by promotion, and gain confidence along with fellow colleague's admiration.

Self Actualization: This reflects on individuals and the way they think about them selves and is measured usually by their potential, success, challenges ahead and also creativity.

Maslow's theory was not intended for the work places and its situations however

it has a great deal of appeal and influence in the world of business. Also this

theory would make managers believe that knowing and finding an employee

work level would lead to finding the correct and suited rewards in which to

reward employees. This will help to motivate them at all costs. It is also known

to be a "problematic management philosophy" because "people do not satisfy

their needs for example the higher levels throughout their work situation

however people do satisfy them through their life as well". This shows managers

across companies will need to have an absolute understanding of the social lives

of the employees according to (Mullins 2002, pg428) and this means that management has to and must look at a balance between work and life.

However Arnold et al (1998) argued Maslow's theory and criticized it for ignoring

"capacity of the people and people that are around those who construct their

own perceptions of needs and how they can be met". Also Beardwell et all (2004

p508) states there are just little evidence that shows support of Maslow's model

and it is also said the model is based on understanding the behaviour of the

middle class workers of the United States where the theory was first undertaken

by Maslow. Therefore because of this argument against the model and theory, it

brings into account the strengths & weaknesses of this theory to back up the

theory itself with the positives and the negatives of the argument made against it.

Below are the strengths and weaknesses.

Strengths:

Helps managers to understand the behaviour of their employees.

Helps to gain an understanding of the right financial and no financial rewards for motivation.

Lastly the theory helps overall of the organization's profitability, efficiency and productivity.

Weaknesses:

The theory lacks driven individuals of arising motivators. For example esteem and self actualization can be questionable relevance due to rewards. Another example of an individual is that if they are unhappy with their colleagues or the organization then they would still be motivated because of the motivational factor which is the rewards.

It is difficult for managers to identify the need levels of the individuals and because of this it can affect them in the work place. Also an employee going on from stage 3 (social needs) to stage 4 (esteem needs) may feel their contributions to be accepted by a higher authority of the organization.

Unsatisfied needs provide most motivation – this is where different individuals want so satisfy different needs at certain times. For example a situation such as an employee who may not be favoured by colleagues may instead be favoured by the managers. This could be because of their work ethic, creative and inventive ideas. In which case the employee should continue to do so and impressing them further would result in the individual going from stage 4 (esteem needs) to stage 5 (self actualization).

The theory is not fully supported and it can be empherically proven through studying so. Also the theory cannot be deemed as 100% true because of the human factors as well as inconsistencies.

The basic needs of individuals would not be required to satisfy -because of a scenario that would suggest based on the theory if an individual is lacking basic amenities or are in a questionable environment then they may not fulfil the higher stages of needs in the hierarchy. However a scenario known as "starving artist" is where their basic needs are not fulfilled but continue to push to gain the fame and recognition of their work they desire. Lastly this scenario shows Maslow's theory may not work every time. This is because it is not impossible for that individual to neglect their well being due to their needs and wants to gain fame and recognition.

An article called Balancing work and life: Not just a matter of time flexibility,

argue that work life balance is not just based on both work & social life only but

also time flexibility. Also it is said that there is a growing awareness of the

difficulties arising based on paid work and family commitments which has

sparked a change of policies in the UK. These policy changes are being made

due to the effects of long working hours which have an effect on parental

responsibilities and their relationships with children a top priority. A study by the

National work life forum suggest that half the fathers in the UK spend less than just 5 minutes in a day of contact with their children and other studies indicate

fathers would like to spend more time with their children. However women's

involvement of paid work has been growing, there has not been much of a

change in household responsibilities. According to Charles and Kerr (1999) they

say that because of the small number changes in household responsibilities,

women therefore are carrying on by undertaking most domestic "chores".

Because of the tensions between work life and domestic commitments has led to

"family friendly schemes" which the government has introduced. The

government are concerned about any negative affects on economy and

relationships of families. Employers want to also link it to the needs of the

employees for greater flexibility with the expanded sources of Labour supply.

However in a short time, there have been arguments that developed about the

desirability of making sure there is a much greater balance between work and

life. Also not just for the parents but also employees in general. In terms of practicality both policies that came about from the argument relates to working

patterns that is flexible.

For example Wers (1998) showed the most common practice for all employees

were that it was having "the ability to switch from full- time to part-time

employment" according to (Cully et al 1999). Also an employer survey based on

work-life balance baseline studies showed results which indicated that most

common practices of employees were having flexibility over both the working

hours and part-time employment. Also a lot of employers because of these

studies have taken action by having temporal flexible working known as flexi-

time which is a response of theirs in order to meet the growing demand of

flexible working by employees. This scheme is beneficial for the employer

themselves because at times so that staff are available to work at extended

period whether it during the week or the day. According to (Bond et al

2002) employers implemented temporal flexible working in order for an increase in staff retention i.e. keeping a hold of their employees in the tight labour

markets. Also according to (Cooper et al 2001), work life balance discussions

have resulted in concentrating specifically on the patterns of working hours and

its extent. However (Cooper et al 2001) stated that given the little attention to

work life debates, it has gone down to a point of qualitative and intangible

factors of the work place that can have a big effect and become involved in the

workers lives itself.

According to a article by emerald insight, talks about organizational strategies to

assist employee retention within the hospitality sector and state how employees

can be retained. In which this article discusses many other research based

studies articles that focus on functional human resource HR activities such as

recruitment and training. For example Collins (2007), Dermondy et el. (2004),

Reynolds et al. (2004) and Martin et al. (2006) all focus on the important

aspects and role in which recruitment plays in by retaining good staff. Also making improvements on the quantity and quality of hospitality staff depends on

the improvement of the image of the industry and organization along with at the

same time having more strategic and effective ways of managing the work rotas

and workloads. Dermody et al argues that staff are hourly paid are mostly

motivated because of staff schemes and incentive pay programmes and cash

bonuses. Flexible working hours are very important for staff motivation along

with mentoring programmes to boost their skills and knowledge so they can

learn to move up to a higher position in the future.

Recruiters in the hospitality sector is suggested to be more aware of different

attributes and skills such as computing and language skills which are required

for during the hotel recruitment. However the (BAS) known as basic allowance

sustenance rates argue that a lot of recruiters are not strategic enough in this

area. Furthermore another HR function which is a retention strategy, which

receives attention in literature, is that of training. According to research done by

Chiang et al 2005, shows the relationships between training, job satisfaction and

also having the intention of remaining within the hospitality industry. Research

suggests that training given was positively related to both job and training

satisfaction as well as to stay within the industry. Education is related to that of

training whereas the type of training given by providers of it such as vocational

institutions and universities.

Also studies undertaken by Hjalager and Andersen (2001) research if

employment in tourism is contingent, temporary and the big question they ask

is if tourism is actually a career. A report by relationships forum Australia by

Shepanski and diamond (2007) state more than 20 per cent of their workers in

the country work around 50 hours per week or more and also 30 per cent work

during the weekend. 2 million Australians spend around 6 hours per week of

family time only on Sundays.

They also state that there are different methods which can be implemented to retain staff and balancing both work and life by the following:

Have flexible working hours including days off and schemes that are family friendly starting and finishing times of work.

Hold training days during work hours

Have the right resources so that employees can do their job properly and best as possible.

Provide flexible arrangements for work based on job sharing and working from home.

Giving employees breaks at work with sufficient amount of time.

Have correct staff numbers so that the work place is not over loaded.

Organizations should have different types of leave.

Employees should be rewarded for their good and hard work.

Special staff events that include their families being included.

And encouraging sound management and its practices.

The recommendations above are to assist organizations to hold on to their best

employees and by also being able to provide a holistic experience which involves

work life balance with the environment of work and private lives. Also doing this,

means turnover of employees can cause overload, stress, & low satisfaction, less commitment from employee but can all be improved along with the retention of

good staff in organizations. In conclusion this review was to look at current

issues of work life balance and find ways or current methods that have been

used by organizations. It has looked at many different materials and publications

of work life balance in which it has created an understanding if organizations can

increase staff retention and improve work life balance. Also by looking at many

publications which gives an in depth look at the different situations that exist on

the basis of work life balance issues.

Many findings were discovered such as the hospitality industry and how it has

incorporated schemes to give employees a balance between work and life. Also

other key findings were for example theories by Maslow, however although

Maslow describes the hierarchy and the stages including its needs, the findings

showed that there are weaknesses according to sources such as Arnold et al

(1998) & Beardwell (2004). This show that the model has negatives along with the positives relating to employees or individuals in a work place. It gives an

indication all theories are not as they seem as they have draw backs. The above

research shows the progression and steps organizations have taken or are

willing to take. These are for example the Shetland NHS who has many

programmes based on work life balance. In doing so successfully, they have a

strong relationship with their employees and giving those employees a better

work life balance.

These are some positives of the research that show there are organizations

introducing programmes however there is still some work to be done across to

have these programmes introduced everywhere just as the Shetland NHS has

done. Organizations must look at their example and see the positive impact of

having work life balance can do especially for their business which is to keep it

functioning along with keeping the best staff from leaving by giving them an

incentive and reason to stay. Also there are many ways if increasing staff retention and improving work life balance as stated however schemes of

development is equally important too in terms of individuals who have

aspirations to progress in their respective organization.

This is a topic that has had many positives found along with negatives that need

to be worked on however it is something that has a lot of feel and demand over

which is to be seen into more thoroughly than this review than it has been

already as there are many ideas how organizations can introduce programmes

and schemes in order to tackle it and find a solution to increase staff retention

and improve work life balance.

Methodology

This project was done using an approach that enabled to create a hypothesis which can be looked at having both quantitative and qualitative results for the data analysis. Having done thorough and extensive secondary data research, it gave an understanding that by having work life balance improved it improves staff retention. This was then reflected in the hypothesis for this for this research which is "By improving work life balance of employees, it will increase retention".

The hypothesis is important and used in this research as it relates to the title of this project. Also the hypothesis linked to the research objectives, those were to:

- Gain opinions of the participants of work life balance
- Opinions of participants about possible policies that should be introduced for work life balance
- Information about flexibility at work
- Views and opinions of current employees about the reasons why work life balance schemes and policies may not have been introduced.

The method used for primary research was to use two companies, one which has work life balance schemes and the other that does not. Also the best form of primary data was the use of a survey i.e. questionnaire and using a questionnaire will help gain a huge amount of data from a lot of people such as current employees who have work life balance and employees without work life balance. Furthermore interviews and focus groups were also used as primary research, these 2 research methods help analysis to be used as qualitative data. The analysis of the questionnaires, focus groups and structured interview can be seen on appendix 1 – focus group 1, appendix 2 – focus group 2, appendix 3 – questionnaire and appendix 4- questionnaire answers and appendix 5 – interview with Mrs. Farzana Miah.

Members of the public in random selection will be asked to participate into completing a questionnaire which the results will be discussed in the findings and analysis section of this research after the results have been gathered. The focus groups were also used for research analysis in order to gain an understanding about work life balance policies which will also help to gain questions that will suitable for the questionnaire itself. The focus group that was conducted and questions asked in the focus group can be seen in appendix 4.

Also the focus groups had 5 participants which consisted of 2 different age groups. The 2 focus groups contained age group of 20-30 and another 40+. The focus groups were set out by having open questions which were answered by each participant. Doing so, it created further discussion about the topic work life balance. Although the focus groups were structured, it was highly productive in which it gave a further insight therefore questions that participants asked can also be looked at thoroughly. All the information and data gained from the focus groups helped to gain understanding about the different views and opinions participants have on work life balance based on the issues of it. A key part of the discussion during the focus group was that whether the participants work life balance was good or if they were either more financial or time based.

The results gathered from the focus groups formed an important base that was needed to create the questions for the questionnaire itself.

Furthermore on the questionnaire, it was created by using a layout of questions which would have helped in gaining as much information from people and creating a positive response rate about the research topic. Some of the elements that were key to creating the right questionnaire were the following.

- Having the most effective and strongest possible questions for people to answer
- The layout of it being precise and clear
- Having a good order of asking each question step by step
- Asking the main questions about the research topic that is intuitive and spontaneous.

Whilst making the questionnaire, it was very clear in doing so because of the ideas gained from the focus groups and the literature review. Also the literature review and focus groups helped form the best questions to have on the questionnaire. Therefore to see how precise, effective and useful the questions asked on the questionnaire would be, there was a sample survey completed. This consisted of 5 participants from a local appliance shop. Doing this sample survey was a fantastic way of seeing how good the response rate of the questionnaire would be and the results from it. The results were very positive as all the 5 participants had mentioned the questionnaire was effective, simplistic and not time constraining to do as each survey to complete took 1 to minutes.

After the sample survey, an official survey was handed to 3 companies and the participants were TK Maxx Balham employees and a local pharmacy in Tooting and Local grocery store. After getting permission of being able to do the research, 30 employees from TK Maxx were given questionnaires, and 10 employees were given questionnaires from the local pharmacy and 7 employees of a grocery store and lastly another 60 members of the general public were given questionnaires to complete. On a negative note permission to hand out the questionnaires was not granted by the owner, Mr. Hussain, as he felt it would be best not to take part so that his employees will not have interests in work life balance issues at their own work place and ask questions about it. However being given permission by store manager of TK Maxx, Michael Phillips and senior pharmacist Mrs. Farzana Miah, i was able to carry out the research required. The remaining questionnaires were given out to the general public.

An interview was conducted with the senior pharmacist, Mrs. Farzana Miah about the pharmacy's stance on work life balance. The interview consisted of getting further information about their policies on work life balance. She was able to give details of the benefits employees and herself have in the company and the negatives there were previously in the company without a strong stance in the policies of work life balance. An example of a positive in the company is employees can take short breaks more so now than before as most employees have a 4 day week job there.

The interview with the senior pharmacist was structured well which was done in a way it would make the participant ask more questions which made the research very effective. The interview transcript with Mrs. Farzana Miah can be seen below on appendix 5.

Findings:

Employees of local pharmacy in tooting, TK Maxx in wands worth and a local grocery store al took part in a questionnaire/survey. The survey was based on the hypothesis which was "improving work life balance of employees, it will increase retention". Altogether there were 100 people taking part from organisations and the general public. All 100 participants took part in the research questionnaire.

Primary research had included many numbers of qualitative research methods; these were structured interviews and focus groups as well as the questionnaire. Research using all of the above methods was done to find and gain an understanding of work life balance of employees and also to get an understanding of any issues that get in the way of their social life because of work. The primary research that was conducted in many forms also looked at if action taken by employers to improve work life balance can increase the retention of staff and being able to keep their key workers.

These are the figures and results of the 100 people that participated based on gender. TK Maxx's participants had 30 employees, 19 of those were male and 11 of those were woman. The 10 employees from the local pharmacy, 6 were women and 4 were men and finally the 60 members of the public consisted 38 males and 22 women. Altogether out of all the participants there were 61 Males and 49 women.

The age groups that participated in completing the questionnaire were the following:

18 or under years of age: 8
18-24 years of age: 14
25-40 years of age: 34
40-55 years of age: 23
55-60 years of age: 12
60 and over years of age: 9

These figures are based on each participant's employment i.e. if the participants are in part time employment or full time employment.
Full time: 78
Part time: 22
The difference between part time and full time workers were that part time workers were not seen as a much of an importance like full time workers based on employment protection. However legislation was made that both part time and full time workers benefit equally in a circumstances. The legislation was made by the European court of Justice in 1997.

Next was the type of sector they work in, i.e. is it public sector or in the private sector. Although TK Maxx employees consisted of 30 are in the public sector as well as the pharmacy which consisted of 10 participants in the questionnaire survey. However besides those two companies, the 60 participants of the general public who were surveyed gave the following results.

Public sector: 38
Private sector: 12

Also the family status of the participants was an important question and analysis that was required for this research because it can help identify the different status's they have with their family. The results from this can garner key information such as the thoughts of work life balance in their company who have family and single parent or single people feelings towards work life balance.

The statistics were:
    Single: 37
    With a partner: 18
    Single parent: 7
    Both partner and children: 38

After doing this part of the survey, it shows that there is a good balance of each category of people's status' that way it helped to find the information required for this research.

The next findings section was about people being affected because of any clashes between their work and life.

    Clash between work and family life: yes: 61
    No clash between work and family life: 39

Furthermore surveyors were asked if their employers and company they work for currently has any work life balance policies.
The results were based on the following policies chosen for this research:

-     Pension scheme: Yes = 76, No = 24
-     Paternity leave: Yes = 84, No = 16
-     Maternity leave: Yes = 100, No = 0
-     Flexible working: Yes = 60 , No = 40

-        Shift work: Yes = 60, No = 40
-        Bonuses: Yes = 34, No = 66

These results show the lack of attention needed to be focused on the people who are unsatisfied with their shift work for instance; this has a percentage of 40% who have answered no.

Also the next question was, if there is a good work life balance in your place of work: 61 answered yes that there is a good work life balance and 39 answered no that there is not a good work life balance. The 39 participants answering no is because they feel their companies lack suitable work life balance policies.

Next question answered by participants in the questionnaire was if they felt there is enough work life balance policies, 45 answered no and 55 answered yes. Some of the participants elaborated in discussion why they felt there are not enough policies. Simply put their most common criticisms were about flexibility, shift work and some who do not have a pension schemes and paternity leave.

Will there be a positive impact on yourself by having work life balance policies was the next question answered. The results were 100 answered yes and 0 answered no. This was a resounding finding as it shows the lack of policies in their favour that would most certainly boost efficiency and motivation within the company and within the employees if they had the policies in the companies.

Also some participants discussed the last question they answered which was, What do you think by having work life balance policies will do for an organisation?, 36 answered it will increase staff retention, 29 answered it will decrease the number of absentees and finally 35 answered it would increase the motivation in employees.

Analysis

This is the analysis of the findings made of each question that was answered by the 100 participants in completing the questionnaire.

By looking at the age groups findings and the results, it is positive that there are many age groups that participated in healthy numbers which helps the research required. It helps in terms of getting many views of the participants about work life balance along with issues or not.

Secondly the results from the questionnaire showed that out of the 22 part time workers who were surveyed, 13 said that their work life balance at work is good and 9 said there needs to be work life balance schemes implemented in their work places because some felt they are not motivated enough because of it and do not feel their social life outside such as family are getting enough of their time. There were 78 full time workers that were surveyed, out of the 78, 49 had responded positively saying their work place had schemes in place that satisfy both their working conditions and meet their needs of their social life and lastly 29 said that they do not feel that there is much of work life balance schemes and incentives because they feel they need those implemented as they have long hours as they are full time workers.

Thirdly participants were asked if they work in a public or private sector. This helps analyse if they certainly are benefitting from work life balance policies in their respective work places. This is because private sector employees that were surveyed do not have the satisfaction of many or any work life balance policies. They claimed they do not receive a pension scheme, emergency leave or maternity pay or bonus especially during Christmas as it is very busy. However public sector employees do get some for example they do have a pension scheme, maternity and paternity leave, emergency leave at conveniences of an employee, discounts on store products, annual leave.

Furthermore in terms of family status, participants who have a partner or a child against the participants, who are single, feel that they have an unbalanced work life. This is because the single workers have less responsibility than those that have a partner or child to support. Also another reason that they feel their hours of work affects their time outside of work to be with their families. In which case if the organisations bought in some work life balance schemes and methods then those workers will feel motivated and work harder knowing it is worth it. This will increase the organisations staff retention and not lose their key workers.

Next was if participants felt there is a clash between their work and life. Looking at the results, the people who have no clashes seem to be more of the single workers as they typically wouldn't have the same commitments that a person with a partner or family does. This shows the dissatisfaction that the 61 people who answered yes have a problem with their work life balance which is not enough for them.

This is a key policy and question about policies currently in their respective companies. It is important in any working environment to have shift work. This is because shift work will be very much a foundation if an employee will have their work and life balanced as they want to have hours with their families. Also the 40% of participants answering no have no flexible working in their opinion. According to Rana (2002) states workers are afraid to ask for hours to be reduced or even to be negotiated to suit their outside life needs as well as balance it with their work. The findings of this part of the research also shows that participants felt they need a better work life balance but are unable to say their wishes or general feelings towards it to the organisation itself.

Participants were asked about if they have a good work life balance. A few participants discussed about the lack of flexible working hours due to family commitments as well as saying they at times have no motivation to work. Maslow (1954) states it is known as "Problematic management philosophy", this would suggest managers face problems because employees will not be motivated and will not work to their full potential as there are clearly problems with some employees that are distracting them.

The next question was based on if their companies have good work life balance policies. Mullins (2002, pg 428) states managers of organisations must be able to understand and recognize the social lives of their employees in order to find a balance of work and life for their employees. Therefore managers must introduce policies that suit their employees and also it will benefit the organisation by keeping a hold of their top workers i.e. increases staff retention. Also by introducing policies, employees will have a fair and rightful work life balance. Participants showed and described their frustrations to the policies they would be like to see introduced that would boost them.

All 100 participants answered yes. This was one of the key questions answered by participants and furthered evidence that work life balance policies must be seen as a necessary ingredient to success and also for employees to have. 100 answering yes no doubt shows how much participants would be motivated, boost their morale, give them a balance so that they can have time with their families and most importantly shift work and incentive policies. Also again Mullins (2002) states all managers across organisations have to see and understand their employee's social lives and situations.

In the last question of the survey about, it proved to be decisive as participants said absentees would be at a decreased level because they need the money to provide for their family however they feel forced to come into work with a weak morale because of the fact that there is not policies that will help them to be with their families as often as they would like. This brings into question why companies do not see this as a necessity and key part of their structure and save on costs of hiring because a lot of people leave to find somewhere more suitable based on time of work, shifts, incentives and of course money and policies.

Conclusion

In conclusion this research, the literature and secondary data linked with work life balance were critically reviewed in order to develop a hypothesis which was developed and tested through the use of primary research and the findings from it.

Also the flexible firm model by (Atkinson 1982), written by Arne L. Kalleberg Dec 2001, has many views on flexibility of work in the 1980's. There were two systems in the flexible firm model known as the numerical flexibility and functional flexibility. Both were explore thoroughly to create an understanding of work life balance and how to improve on it. This model developed by Atkinson in 1982 was done to be the solution of a working environment. Also organisations could use this model by putting their operations based on the model and improve on production and versatility in a work place.

Using this model can also help develop an understanding between the company and employees especially what the employees want and what the company wants. The model provides methods to help boost improvement in all areas, team working ethics and organisations can meet their strategic objectives.

An article on job characteristics theory of motivation by J Richard Hackman and GR Oldham, state how factors of jobs link with the satisfaction of employees and their attendance. There were certain characteristics that affected the behaviour and attitudes of individuals at a work place. The theory showed that individuals with a need of high growth were affected more because of changed in job characteristics. In which an employee's motivation is important depending on their needs of wanting to grow and develop individually.

Also it was founded that when an individual has a strong motive to develop and grow then the more their motivation increases as long as their feelings which become more positive. This leads to positive performance. There are key elements that increase motivation, performance at work and satisfaction of their job. These elements are the significance of the task which elevates the jobs importance, autonomy is based on giving independence to the employees for things such as organising their work as well as scheduling. The other elements are Identity of their task in which it is the unity of the job itself. This is based on a job using a collective approach to do tasks. Lastly skills variety is a key element as it gives employees the chance to use multiple skills, this is essential especially for the individuals wanting to grow and develop. Finally Feedback is a great way for employees to know how they are doing and knowing the quality of their performance in the job.

The characteristic approach theory looks at job design and it also focuses on key elements such as characteristics that affect social relationships of employees, therefore respective organisations can increase work life balance of their employees especially those that have children and partners.

Another essential and important theory of motivation is the psychological contract. This was first bought into fruition in the early 1960's. This theory is based on elements such as the effort performance relationship, performance reward relationship and rewards personal goals relationship. Therefore employees will be highly motivated to reach a high level of effort when that effort goes and leads up to performance appraisal. Also the psychological contract is seen as looking at the reality of situations and could be more of an influence than a typical formal contract in affecting how an employee behaves. The main aspect of this is that it brings the two parties together who agree on promises and obligations mutually. For example some of the obligations will be about job security, flexibility, salary and loyalty. Mullins (2002), states that promises and obligations are an important part of an employees experience and this is where the psychological contract theory takes full effect because when those promises and obligations are met, the employee's motivation level is at a high as well as their performance.

Also secondary data that was researched such as published material i.e. articles, journals, gave a clear examples of work life balance in organisations for example the Shetland NHS are a great example of providing their employees with a work life balance that suits their needs both outside and inside of work. This has had a great effect because it has increased staff retention. This shows that other organisations can follow the Shetland NHS and see how have developed a work life balance programme that works.

Furthermore the motivation theories such as Maslow hierarchy of needs, Herzberg and Job characteristics approach theory all show that why it is important for organisations to implement a good work life balance scheme. There are clearly good examples how it can be done successfully like the Shetland NHS and also the Lloyds Pharmacy, Northampton.

Primary research that was undertaken through the use of questionnaires and focus groups had given results that were clear enough to say employees were in need of shift work and flexible working hours which was the most discussed by participants as they have commitments to their family. The methodology itself was very effective and efficient in the way research was done given the time period initially. The sample survey that was carried out could have been done more extensively which would have helped to cut down on the demand characteristics however the sample survey was a success as it gave a indication of the response rate that would be gained from the official surveying.

The focus groups and interview all gave results that were very good in which they were thorough and had ideas of what employees wanted and issues they have with work life balance policies. The focus groups gave personal opinions of individuals who have positives and negatives about work life balance policies in place at their work place. There were good insights how policies are needed without question as for example Naser Ali was one of the key interviewees because he had no work life balance at all as there were no policies at all, this begged a question, why is there not a legislation of all work places having work life balance policies and regard it as a must?. Also the results that were gained from the questionnaire were described and analysed to create conclusions between the literature review and conclusion itself. However there were discrepancies if work life balance issues actually improve motivation for performance of employees or whether there is an increase in motivation for staff retention.

Participants answered "what do you think by having work life balance policies will do for an organisation?" 36 answered it will increase staff retention, 29 answered it will decrease the number of absentees 35 answered it would increase the motivation in employees. This was a key question and the findings were important as it showed by having work life balance policies, there will be an increase in motivation along with staff retention due to it. This was discussed with the participants and some stated that because of this, individuals would consider long term stay within their current organisations which will suit them indefinitely.

Lastly the main conclusion found in this research overall was that work life balance indeed has a great affect on staff retention which was concluded upon using the results from the focus groups and questionnaires as well as an increase in motivation. However even through critical analysis of the research methods it questioned the reliability as well as the validity of the results gathered because of the discrepancies. Also organisations structure of work life balance policies that ideally improved relationships between the organisation and employees for example the Shetland NHS, were the most effective way for staff to remain in the organisation creating an increase in staff/job retention.

Through the findings of all the research methods used as well as the conclusion were evaluated thoroughly which drew recommendations.

Recommendations

One of the researched organisations was TK Maxx. This organisation has a few work life balance policies such as a pension scheme, maternity leave. However this is not enough as some discussed their issues that the working hours are not flexible enough. Also the employees do not have enough days off as each employee i.e. the part time sales associates only have 11 days off which they feel is unfair as the full time workers have 21 days off.

The best method for TK Maxx to go ahead and listen to their employees is by researching the needs of their employees before implementing any other work life balance policies. This can be done by using a day to hold a focus group and survey consisting solely of their employees so that the issues can be seen and understood. It is very important for the management department to gather data that will be effective and crucial before any changes are made especially for those who have a child, partner and a family. This is because those are the most influenced by the current work life balance policies at TK Maxx as some associates showed and discussed their frustration of not enough family time and lack of time off when required.

Furthermore Nasar Ali of focus group 1, a chef in Radha Krishna restaurant had said there is no policies at all, therefore an individual with no policies of work life balance struggles with work hours with no flexibility, time off when needed to attend a family matter, maternity leave, paternity leave and bonuses as the head chef is given. The organisation must understand his needs as he is not motivated and the morale is at a low. Therefore amendments must be made similarly to TK Maxx by possibly undertaking a focus group and survey to identify the issues they have and policies they want to be implemented.

Organisations as a whole also need to have an understanding that it will take time to understand those needs of employees and to fully establish the correct policies that will satisfy them because every individual have different needs. Also the organisations need to show their commitment towards work life balance. Also importantly the employees need to be shown that there will indeed be a good work life balance. This will increase the motivation and morale of employees meaning increase in staff retention.

Also the management departments of organisation should involve their staff of making the new work life balance schemes and policies. This is a great method that can be used in the employers favour because it will give them knowledge on the types of work life balance policies that are available to them and how they can be implemented. All organisations should have an open minded approach about work life balance policies because there will be demands everywhere for those policies by employees and also the government. If organisations can take away any critical or negative feelings towards work life balance then there will be a boost in being able to get skilled and very highly experienced workers to work for the organisation from all over the globe. This will increase morale and boost credentials of the organisations.

Also employees must learn and understand everything about the policies so that those employees can relate those needs they have to their supervisors or management in order to understand the employee's needs and tailor any changes to those needs. Furthermore regular training sessions and meetings which would be very beneficial so that any work life balance policies will be known as best as possible by staff and management and if any future amendments are required.

There must be a commitment by organisations to multi skilling because instead of having a few employees doing the highly skilled tasks, there can be more employees with the right training and commitment who can all do the same. This will give employees a goal to aim for as well as motivation because of being given the chance to learn something new and valuable to move up in a company, this is where the characteristic approach of motivation comes in. Another positive factor of this would be that the current multi skilled worker who has long hours can have shorter hours and use that extra time with their families while the employees in training come up the ranks and learn.

Lastly after making these recommendations, Organisations should and will have an increase in staff retention with the implementation of the recommendations given. The recommendations give thorough and multiple ways of doing so with the uses of work life balance policies. Also organisations must not forget to support their staff in every way possible within every department of an organisation which will increase motivation levels as well as build morale within the working environment. The recommendations given are not the only source required for organisations but also they need to look into other organisations such as Lloyds Pharmacy where Mrs. Farzana Miah is employed or a great example of work life balance policies in the Shetland NHS who have a superb policy implementation throughout which has been done so very successfully by focusing on the needs of all of their staff which creates positive morale, increase in staff retention and a motivated work force.

Appendices:

Appendix 1: Focus Group 1

Hi there i am Jabeir Ahmed. This will be conducted for your views and opinions of work life balance.

Could I please have your names and your current role and organisation you are currently an employee of.

1.   Farzana Miah, 2. Naser Ali, 3. Sunny Kuttan, 4. Delilah Roberts, 5. Shabir Islam.

1- Name: Farzana Miah and I work for Lloyd's pharmacy in Northampton as a senior pharmacist.

2- Name: Naser Ali, My profession is a chef at Radha Krishna restaurant in London.

3- Name: Sunny Kuttan, cricket coach at Surrey cricket club.

4- Name: Delilah Roberts, i am a hairdresser at Scissors and Style salon in London

5- Name: Shabir Islam, Sales associate at Marks and Spencer's in Royal Docks, London

Please say the work life balance schemes there are at your respective work places.

1-   Flexible work days, 21 days off a year, Gym membership and maternity leave.

2-   None at all, except paid holiday.

3-   Gym membership, 1 month annual leave during off season, free meals at club house.

4-   Free hair cuts, Discounts on all hair products, maternity leave.

5-   Free lunch, also 20% discount on all items in store, paid leave for 21 days.

Which policies affect you and would create job satisfaction?

1-   The salary that i get and the days off are probably enough to satisfy me as i can take days off as i have a family.

2-   I just feel that if there were policies that other employees of other companies have then id be much more enthusiastic and motivated to give it my all.

3-   As a coach i do get quite a few perks such as the annual leave, and quick progression up the ladder to coach older aged players. My job is very flexible as well as i do not have to work 5 days a week like everyone else but 2-3 days a week with a good pay packet and also a recreational room i can use at any time which is great,

4- The satisfaction i get from the salon is okay, i wouldn't say the best although i do get an employee discount however al employees do in their own work places i guess. In my opinion it can be better.

5- I am satisfied some what, but i am happy with the fact that i do get discount, as Marks and Spencer's is really good, however they could improve on pay, and possibly better working hours, i have a family to support and as a sales associate i feel there should be more policies to support myself and my other sales associate colleagues.

What policies of work life balance would you want to see introduced in your work place?

1- There could be more training given to the newer employees, also there could be days to review performances and give bonuses, of course this is beneficial in order to reward someone for hard work.

2- I would like to see bonuses given, as well as flexible working hours and not just fixed hours, a lot of us have families so id want to be around them too, not just on my day off, it is not enough.

3- I feel the perks and policies i have available to me are fantastic i could not ask for anymore.

4-	I would have liked to have more policies based on paid holiday incentives, or days off of certain days in the week to be with my family without having my bonus reduced. Also it would be great to have shift work where i would be able to change my work hours with another colleague if an emergency or commitment outside arises.

5-	During my hour break, there isn't much i can do in terms of a employee lounge, for example my mate who works in Tesco, says that they have a small pool table and a vending machine.

If your work places had the policies and schemes you would like to be introduced, then would you feel satisfied?

1-	The way things are at this moment in time is okay, not particularly the best however i refer to training again, in order to have a reason to stay id like to be given more training myself and others should be given training that way we understand everything about our work place so we can progress one day to a higher position. We want targets and goals especially opportunities.

2-	I would certainly feel more motivated if these were in place as i would have a objective to work towards something and feel rewarded.

3-	I am pleased with the current policies in place right now; it is simply amazing that i can enjoy a career in the sport of football while enjoying these policies too so i can spend time with my family too.

4-   At on point i felt i needed to move on to have a better chance to earn more money to support myself, however i was given a chance to do a colour degree which would boost my earnings in completion i was told and have a pension scheme. So therefore i am not sure but I am more over on staying and doing the degree.

5-   Overall i am happy with the work and hours but feel there should be more for us employees to do on our breaks as other companies have. Recreational things in place would be a stimulus and also id like it if there were more opportunities to climb up the hierarchy as i have been here for nearly 3 years.

That is it for this focus group, thank you so much to all for your time and effort taken to participate in this.

Appendix 2: Focus group 2:

Focus Group 2:

Hi there i am Jabeir Ahmed. This will be conducted for your views and opinions of work life balance.

Could I please have your names and your current role and organisation you are currently an employee of.

1 – Name: Abdul Kaium – I work at a local cab office as a cab driver

2 - Name: Keeran – I am a retail operative/assistant at Primark in Tooting Broadway store

3 – Name: Assam Ahmad – A graphic designer at Fast Printing Ltd.

4: - Name: Paul Branning – sales advisor at WHSmith in Tandem shopping centre in Colliers Wood.

5 – Name: Derek Bradley – Manager of Barratt's shoes in Southside shopping centre located in Wandsworth.

Could you please state the work-life balance schemes you are aware of, that your organisation has in place?

1- As i am a cab driver, i am self employed meaning i a can work at any time and take days off when ever i want which gives me a peace of mind to be with my family any time.

2- Since I'm just a part time worker on weekends only, i don't get the benefits i would typically as a full time worker would as i work just 4 hours each day, but i do have flexible hours, as well as i can take a day off if needed which helps because i am a student.

3- Company policies available to me are flexible working hours, 2 days off in the weekend along with 1 optional day off during the weekday.

4- I am not aware of any company policies because I am still under a temporary contract as I am on probation typically for a new staff member for the first 3 months.

5- As a manager I do get a lot of benefits from the polices that include days off whenever i choose, flexible working, company discounts, gym membership.

If your work places had the policies and schemes you would like to be introduced, then would you feel satisfied?

1 – As i am self employed as a can driver i do not feel like i am actually missing anything in terms of policies. The main policy for me has always been to have flexible work hours and work any time that suits me which is great.

2 - Even though i am part time employee with short hours, i always hoped i could finish a little earlier on a Sunday or at least have my shift changed to a earlier start and finish because that way i can avoid traffic at congestion hours. None the less i am happy with the working hours in general and the flexibility of work.

3- I am very much happy with the policies the company has, it brings great satisfaction and a delight to work in a field that i love as well as having policies that go with it to have a balance between work and life outside of work.

4 - As far as policies go, i would definitely like to see a change where even temporary staff on probation receives

the same benefits of policies but i am satisfied with the way things are.

5 – As a manager i feel i get the most out of my work place in terms of flexibility and a balance between my work and life. I personally feel very happy as i am and with the current structure in place of policies. However i would like to see more training given by the company for the sales advisors, in which i have taken initiative to ask the area manager on their behalf. This would help for them to push on for a better position.

What policies of work life balance would you want to see introduced in your work place?

1- Something that creates better communication, away from work, maybe voice mail when away on holiday.

2- I would like to have had more overtime but i do understand I am not the only person after overtime, but seeing as i have weekend hours of 4 per day i need the extra hours as i do have bills and other payments.

3- As i am a graphic designer, i am very much happy in every way with the policies in place, but i would personally like training to move up the ladder in terms of better salary. My current pay package is not the best as i do have a family to support but all in all the policies are very good.

4- Any policies or schemes because currently i do not benefit from any schemes or policies because of my status working as a temporary staff on probation which i feel is unfair given the salary i am on too.

5- I am a manager who has been lucky enough to work as a manager, therefore all the policies and schemes available to me are perfect and would not personally want anymore than i already have in place.

That is it for this focus group, thank you so much for your time participating to help me with my research.

Appendix 3: Questionnaire:

Questionnaire for work life balance:

Please place a tick next to your answers.

Question 1: please specify gender:

- Male:
- Female:

Question 2: Age group:

- 18 years old or below:
- 18-24:
- 25-40:
- 40-55:
- 55-60:
- 60 years and over:

Question 3: Mode of work:

- Part time:
- Full time:

Question 4: Hours of work each week:

- 8 to 16 hours:
- 16-25hours:
- 25-40 hours:
- Over 40 hours:

Question 5: Family:

- Single:
- Partner:
- Single parent:
- Both partner and children:

Question 6: Is there a clash between work and family life?

- Yes:
- No:

Question 7: Sector working in currently:

- Public sector:
- Private sector:

Question 8: Work life balance policies Your company currently has:

- Pension scheme:
- Paternity leave:
- Maternity leave:
- Flexible working:
- Shift work available:
- Bonuses:

Question 9: Is there a good work life balance in your place of work:

- Yes:
- No:

Question 10: Has your work impacted

negatively on your outside life:

- Yes:
- No:

Question 11: Is there enough work life balance policies that satisfy you?

- Yes:
- No:

Question 12: will there be a positive impact On yourself by having work life balance:

- Yes:
- No:

Question 13: what do you think by having work life balance will do for an organisation:

- Have a positive impact on motivation of the workers?
- Improve on staff retention?
- Decrease worker being absent?

Appendix 4: Questionnaire results summary:

Please specify your gender:
Male: 61
Female: 39
Please select the age group you fall into?
18 or under years of age: 8
18-24 years of age: 14
25-40 years of age: 34
40-55 years of age: 23
55-60 years of age: 12
60 and over years of age: 9

What is your mode of work?

Full time: 78

Part time: 22
Sector working in currently?
Public sector: 38
Private sector: 12

Your family life/situation?

Single: 37
With a partner: 18
Single parent: 7
Both partner and children: 38

Is there a clash between work and family life?

Clash between work and family life: yes: 61
No clash between work and family life: 39

Work life balance policies your company currently has?

Pension scheme: Yes = 76, No = 24
Paternity leave: Yes = 84, No = 16
Maternity leave: Yes = 100, No = 0
Flexible working: Yes = 60, No = 40
Shift work: Yes = 60, No = 40
Bonuses: Yes = 34, No = 66

Is there is a good work life balance in your place of work?

Yes: 61

No: 39

Are there enough work life balance policies?

Yes: 55

No: 45

Will there be a positive impact on you by having work life balance policies.

Yes: 100

No: 0

What do you think by having work life balance policies will do for an organisation?

36 answered it will increase staff retention

29 answered it will decrease the number of absentees

35 answered it would increase the motivation in employees.

Appendix 5: Interview transcript with Mrs Farzana Miah:

My self: "What does having work life balance policies mean to you?"

Mrs. Miah: "Work life balance gives my self and my colleagues a peace of mind where you feel comfortable at work and motivated knowing you also have enough time outside of work.

My self: "Thank you, so what policies are currently available in the pharmacy?"

Mrs. Miah: "As i said in the focus group, we the pharmacy has 21 days off a year, maternity leave, as well as flexible working days which are really good and staff training sessions."

My self: "Very good, also do these policies meet your needs and requirement of work life balance?"

Mrs. Miah: "I feel the flexible working days and 21 days off a year is absolutely brilliant because i have a son and husband which are my most important commitment, those policies help be with them and take days off in case of a emergency or in general."

My self: "Would you like to see any other policies implemented in the pharmacy?"

Mrs. Miah: "I mean everyone has different needs, but i feel that I'm very much satisfied with the current policies as well as having training sessions to develop and for a move up the ladder and also better pay."

My self: "I understand some other participants complained about having no training or added incentive of being trained so they can move up to a better position and pay, therefore how do you feel this policy has gone for you so far?"

Mrs. Miah: "Well that is one of the great things about this pharmacy because training is given regularly and also i completed a course in pharmaceuticals level 3 NVQ funded by the pharmacy itself. It was great for me as i became a senior pharmacist where my salary also increased. This career move has been fantastic because i can support my family as best as i can."

My self: "Mrs. Miah what would you change and why based on work life balance policies of course?"

Mrs. Miah: "Well to be honest i have no disgruntles or problems with how the pharmacy is run in terms of the policies they have in this establishment, i have no issues at all about these policies, i feel personally that the key policies are already in place which is why the pharmacy is running smoothly with motivated workers."

My self: "Mrs. Miah i would like to say a big thank you to you for taking the time out for me to conduct this interview. Your answers and insight about the policies and pharmacy has given me a lot of valuable information. Also again thank you.

Mrs. Miah: "Fantastic i was able to help and the pleasure was all mine, thank you."

Bibliography:

- RANA (2002)

• Alan Chapman. (2001-2010). *Frederik Herzberg motivation theory.*Available: http://www.businessballs.com/herzberg.htm. Last accessed 20th October.

• Andrew Neher. (1991). Journal of humanistic psycology. *Maslows theory of motivation: A critique.* 31 (3), 89-112.

• Anne Hjalager & Steen Andersen . (2001). *Tourism employment: contingent work or professional career.* Available: http://www.emeraldinsight.com/journals.htm?articleid =879744&show=abstract. Last accessed 29th August.

• Arnold, J. and Randall, R. (2010) Work Psychology, 5th edn, London: FT Pearson, Chap on Work motivation in course text.

• Arne L. Kalleberg. (December 2001). *Organizing flexibility: the flexible firm in a new century.* Available: https://ulib.derby.ac.uk/ecdu/courseres/dbs/manapeo p/kalleberg.pdf. Last accessed 20th October.

• Arrey Mbongaya Ivo. (2006). *Best perspectives of human resource management.* Available: http://www.africancentreforcommunity.com/articles- Dateien/Best%20Perspectives%20to%20human%20re source%20management%20by%20Arrey%20Mbongay a%20Ivo.pdf. Last accessed 8th sept 2013.

- Business Balls. (2010-2013). *The psychological contract.* Available: http://www.businessballs.com/psychological-contracts-theory.htm. Last accessed 21st October.

- David Shoesmith. (2012). *Flexible working.* Available: http://www.theworkfoundation.com/Research/Workforce-Effectiveness/Good-Work/Flexible-Working. Last accessed 30th Aug 2013.

- Douglas Merrill . (2012). *Dont balance work and life, integrate them.* Available: http://www.forbes.com/sites/douglasmerrill/2012/07/19/dont-balance-work-and-life-integrate-them/. Last accessed 28th August.

- Duane Schultz and Sydney Ellen Schultz, *Psychology and Work Today,* Pearson.

- Emerald insight. (2002). *Building relationships for retention: How Time Warner Cable improves employee engagement.* Available: http://www.emeraldinsight.com/journals.htm?articleid=1793534. Last accessed 26th aug 2013, Strategic direction, Vol. 25 iss: 7.

- Evelina Rog, Julia Christensen Hughes. (2008). *A strategy for improving employee recruitment, retention and engagement within hospitality organizations.* Available: http://www.emeraldinsight.com/journals.htm?articleid=1747878. Last accessed 3rd sept 2013, Vol 20.

- Family and parenting institute. (2011). *Family friendly scheme.* Available: http://www.familyandparenting.org/our_work/Launch +of+Nationwide+Family+Friendly+Scheme. Last accessed 1st sept 2013.

- Human resource management international digest (2002). *Hertfordshire county council: work life balance scheme wins award.* USA: MCB UP LTD. p7-11.

- Institute of management. (2012). *Using the job characteristics theory to motivate employees.* Available: http://m360.sim.edu.sg/article/Pages/Job-Characteristics-Theory-to-Motivate-Employees.aspx. Last accessed October 2013.

- Jonathan Yong. (2012). *The limitations of maslos heirarchy of needs.*Available: http://communicatesmart.blogspot.co.uk/2012/03/limi tations-of-maslows-hierarchy-of.html. Last accessed 10th september.

- Magaret Deery. (2008). *Talent management, work-life balance and retention strategies, Emerald 20.* Available: http://www.emeraldinsight.com/case_studies.htm/jou rnals.htm?articleid=1747881&show=html&WT.mc_id= alsoread. Last accessed 7th september.

- Maslow, A. (1943) 'A Theory of Motivation', Psychological Review, 50: 370-96.

- Melissa Abercromby. (2007). *Importance of work life balance.* Available: http://www.bia.ca/articles/AReportontheImportanceof Work-LifeBalance.htm. Last accessed 26th august.

- Mullins, L. (2010) Management and Organizational Behaviour, 9th edn, London: FT Prentice Hall, pp. 259-68.

- Mullins 2002 psychological theory, Last accessed 18th November
- NHS Shetland. (October 2009). *Work life balance policy.* Available: http://www.shb.scot.nhs.uk/board/policies/hr-WorkLifeBalancePolicy.pdf. Last accessed 28th September.

- Paul Shepanski and Michael Diamond. (2007). *An Unexpected Tragedy: Evidence for the connection between working patterns and family breakdown in Australia.* Available: http://www.relationshipsforum.org.au/report/. Last accessed 8th sept 2013.

- Redman, T. and Matthews, B. (1998). Service quality and human resource management: A review and research agenda.

- Sean Mcleod. (2007). *Maslows heirarchy of needs.* Available: http://www.simplypsychology.org/maslow.html. Last accessed 8th sept 2013.